C0-DAL-985

DISCARD

RAINTREE BIOGRAPHIES

Lewis and Clark

Mary Stout

RAINTREE
Steck-Vaughn
PUBLISHERS

A Harcourt Company

New York

Published by Raintree Steck-Vaughn Publishers, an imprint of Steck-Vaughn Company.

Project Editors: Sean Dolan, Sarah Jameson
Production Manager: Richard Johnson
Designed by Ian Winton
Picture Researcher: Rachel Tisdale

Planned and produced by Discovery Books

Library of Congress Cataloging-in-Publication Data
Available upon request.

ISBN 0-7398-5677-4

Printed and bound in China
1 2 3 4 5 6 7 8 9 0 07 06 05 04 03 02

Acknowledgments 4373
The publishers would like to thank the following for permission to reproduce their pictures:
Cover: Independence National Historical Park; p.4 Bridgeman Art Library; p.5 (left and right) Peter Newark's Western
Americana; p.6 Peter Newark's American Pictures; p.7 Library of Congress; p.8 Peter Newark's American Pictures; p.9 Yale
Collection of Western Americana, Beinecke Rare Book and Manuscript Library; p.10 Peter Newark's American Pictures; p.11
Mary Evans Picture Library/Hamilton Smith Naturalists Library; p.12 Peter Newark's Western Americana; p.13 The
American Numismatic Society; pp.14, 15, 16 & 17 Peter Newark's American Pictures; p.18 Corbis; p.19 Peter Newark's
American Pictures; p.20 Corbis; pp.21 & 22 Peter Newark's Western Americana; p.23 Corbis; p.24 Peter Newark's American
Pictures; p.25 Mary Evans Picture Library; p.27 Peter Newark's American Pictures; p.28 & 29 Corbis.
Map on p.26 by Stefan Chabluk.

Dedication
With thanks to Keaton Renta, Kyla Renta, and Sarah Taubman for their assistance.

CONTENTS

THE PACIFIC OCEAN

On November 7, 1805, explorer William Clark wrote in his journal with elk-hide covers: "Great joy in camp: we are in view of the ocean, this great Pacific Ocean which we [have] been so long anxious to see."

Between 1804 and 1806, captains Meriwether Lewis and William Clark traveled on a voyage of discovery for 19 months across the United States, from east to west and back again.

Everyone was excited, though they were wet, cold, tired, and hungry. This group, known as the "Corps of Discovery," had traveled 4,000 miles (6,400 km), by boat and often on foot and horseback, to reach the Pacific Ocean. They had spent over a year navigating dangerous rivers, wide plains, and high mountains to reach this point in their journey. They had met numerous Native American tribes along the way and encountered many threats in the wilderness.

Lewis (right) and Clark (above) were well chosen as expedition leaders. They both knew how to live in the woods. Lewis was chief planner and scientist; Clark led the men in their daily work and made the maps for the journey.

As the first white Americans to venture across North America to the Pacific west coast, they had no maps to guide them. Instead, they made the first map of the land as they traveled through it.

The leaders of the Corps, or troop, Meriwether Lewis and William Clark, had been chosen by President Thomas Jefferson to explore this new land and find an easy east–west river route. They kept detailed notes of their experiences and discoveries in their journals.

BEFORE THE EXPEDITION

Meriwether Lewis was born on August 18, 1774, and grew up on a plantation in Virginia. He lived only a short distance from the future president, Thomas Jefferson. When he was 20 years old, he became a soldier. The following year, he met an officer named William Clark, and they became good friends. Lewis left the army when he was 27 to work as Thomas Jefferson's private secretary. By then, Jefferson was the new president of the United States.

Thomas Jefferson had been interested in the American frontier since childhood. The Louisiana Purchase he made as president (1801–1809) more than doubled the territory of the young republic. He could now fulfill his wish for an expedition to the West.

William Clark was born on August 1, 1770, in Caroline County, Virginia. He was the ninth of ten children.

Jefferson gave Lewis detailed instructions for the journey. He told Lewis to meet with the Native Americans in friendship, and to arrange for some chiefs to visit him in Washington, D.C. This is a detail from Jefferson's letter to Lewis, dated June 20, 1803.

In 1803 the United States bought from France a large amount of land between the Mississippi River and the Rocky Mountains. This was called the Louisiana Purchase. Jefferson asked Lewis to lead a group of men to explore this new territory, and the lands beyond. Lewis agreed to head the Corps of Discovery, with his friend Clark as co-captain.

Lewis was now 29 years old. He was very smart, but also quiet and shy. Clark was 33 years old with red hair and a cheerful, friendly personality. They were very different people, but worked well as a team. Together they led the Corps of Discovery to the Pacific Ocean and back, with plenty of adventures on the way.

THE JOURNEY PREPARATIONS

Lewis and Clark spent a long time getting ready for their trip. In March 1803, before the Louisiana Purchase was completed, Lewis went to Philadelphia to study plants and animals at the University of Pennsylvania. He studied astronomy so he could navigate through unknown territory by the stars, and medicine so he could look after his team in the wilderness.

Lewis was in charge of building special boats for the trip. The expedition's keelboat was 55 feet (17 m) long with 20 oars for rowing, as well as a sail. Two smaller canoe-like boats called "pirogues" were also made for the trip.

The expedition's special keelboat would have looked something like this one. It could hold 10 tons of supplies, carry 25 people, and be rowed or pulled with ropes by men walking on shore.

PROVISIONS FOR THE TRIP

Lewis wrote list after list of provisions to take, spending $2,500 on almost 2 tons of goods and equipment for the expedition. These included 15 rifles, 176 pounds (80 kg) of gunpowder, 150 yards (137 m) of cloth for making tents and sheets, 12 pounds (5 kg) of soap, 3 bushels (105 liters) of salt, mosquito curtains, writing paper, ink, crayons, compasses, and a traveling library of reference books. In order to trade with the Native Americans, the expedition also packed 12 dozen pocket mirrors, 4,600 sewing needles, 144 pairs of scissors, 130 rolls of tobacco, and 33 pounds (15 kg) of tiny colored beads. Below is just one page of Lewis's many lists.

TRAINING CAMP

While Lewis was studying and having the boats built, Clark hired and trained the recruits for the Corps of Discovery. Then everyone gathered near St. Louis, Missouri, at Camp Wood, where they built a small fort. Here they spent the winter of 1803–1804 learning the skills they would need on the expedition.

Lewis and Clark recruited fearless, strong, mostly unmarried men who would work hard and get along with others. Skills such as hunting, carpentry, and blacksmithing were valuable. They also needed men who could navigate boats and interpret the Native American languages.

When the expedition stopped for the night, the men slept in tents. But when they stopped for the winter, the men had to build a fort, and then build huts inside the fort to live in. In this illustration by Patrick Gass (one of the Corps), the men are busy constructing a wooden hut.

Lewis's dog, Seaman, was a Newfoundland somewhat similar in appearance to this one. Seaman had adventures of his own on the journey, including being kidnapped by Indians!

The recruits were paid $10 per month and given clothing, food, and shelter. They were also promised some land out west after they returned from the trip.

There were up to 45 members in the expedition party in the beginning, and many of them were soldiers.

SOME MEMBERS OF THE CORPS

- York, William Clark's African-American slave
- George Shannon, youngest member (age 17), hunter
- Pierre Cruzatte, boatman, fiddle player and blind in one eye
- Patrick Gass, carpenter; published an illustrated journal of the expedition in 1807
- Toussaint Charbonneau, interpreter
- Sacagawea, a Native American from the Shoshone tribe, and only woman on the trip; wife of Charbonneau
- Seaman, a large, black Newfoundland dog; squirrel hunter, and guard

SETTING OFF

On May 14, 1804, the Corps of Discovery set off in their boats up the Missouri River. During the day, the men would row or, if windy, put up the sails. If the river was too low, the men had to get out and pull the boat forward with ropes. Usually, Clark was in charge of the boats and Lewis walked on shore, looking for new plants and animals to describe and draw in his journal.

The painting Into the Unknown, *by J. K. Ralston, shows the Corps in the course of its long and dangerous journey. The only man that didn't return home was Sergeant Charles Floyd, who died early in the expedition from appendicitis in Iowa.*

Lewis and Clark took mirrors, cloth, tobacco, and beads as gifts for the Native Americans they met. Only the chiefs were given peace medals, which depicted an image of President Jefferson on the front and hands of friendship on the back.

Hunters were sent ashore to kill animals as the boats went along. One day, young George Shannon went hunting and got lost. He spent 16 days alone in the wilderness before he finally rejoined the expedition.

At night, the boats stopped for the men to make camp. Wood was gathered for a fire, and a deer or wild turkey cooked over the flames. The men ate and talked about the day. Some wrote in their journals. Others mended their clothes or made new moccasins out of animal hides. Sometimes repairs were made to the boats, because branches or rocks in the river had damaged them.

Biting Insects

"The mosquitoes and ticks are numerous and bad."

Entry in William Clark's journal, June 17, 1804

CAMP MANDAN

The Corps of Discovery continued up the Missouri River all through the summer and fall of 1804. As winter came upon the expedition, they realized they needed a winter camp, since traveling would become difficult and dangerous. They built a small fort close to a Mandan Indian village, near where Bismarck, North Dakota, is today. They called it "Camp Mandan."

The Mandan Indians lived in two villages on the banks of the Missouri River. Along with their neighbors the Hidatsu, they numbered about 4,000 persons, the largest Native American community the Corps encountered along the Missouri.

The Mandan Indians lived in homes built of wood and earth. They were not nomadic, but stayed in the same place year round. They grew crops of corn, beans, and squash, and twice a year hunted buffalo. The Corps traded with them for food and other items necessary to get through the winter.

This is a portrait of Mato-Tope, a Mandan chief, painted by Karl Bodmer in 1834. The chief has war paint on his body. The hand painted on his chest shows that he took some prisoners during war.

The Mandans and the Corps became good neighbors, and during the long winter they would entertain each other in the evenings. The fiddle music of Pierre Cruzatte was especially popular. York was fascinating to the Mandans, because they had never seen a black man before.

During their stay at Camp Mandan, Lewis and Clark hired a new recruit. He was a French-Canadian fur trader, now living with the Mandans, who wanted work as an interpreter. Toussaint Charbonneau joined the Corps along with his young Shoshone Indian wife, Sacagawea (pronounced Sah-cah'gah-we-ah).

INDIAN COUNTRY

The land that the Corps of Discovery explored wasn't empty, but inhabited by thousands of Native Americans from many different tribes. Lewis and Clark met nearly 50 different tribes on their trip, and usually offered them gifts and peace medals from the president.

Native American nations helped the Corps many times and saved their lives on more than one occasion. The Mandans supplied corn, beans, and squash, the Shoshones sold them horses and guided them along the trails, while the Nez Percé helped the Corps make canoes.

The Bull Dance in a Mandan Village *is the title of this painting by George Catlin (1833). The dance celebrated the ritual testing the endurance and discipline of the young men of the tribe as an entrance to manhood.*

Other nations were less friendly. The Teton Sioux wanted one of the Corps' boats as payment for passing through their land, and the Blackfeet tried to steal their supplies and horses on the way home.

SACAGAWEA, THE SHOSHONE

Who was Sacagawea? Only 17 years old and wife to the Corps' interpreter, she gave birth to her son, nicknamed "Pomp," at Camp Mandan. Sacagawea was a Shoshone who had been stolen from her tribe by the Hidatsa Indians.

Her knowledge of the country, the people, and the food was important for the success of the expedition. Several times when the Corps was lost, she knew the right route to follow. Very little is known about what happened to her after the journey ended.

This painting shows Sacagawea in the mountains with Lewis and Clark. It was painted long after the expedition took place.

TO GREAT FALLS AND BEYOND

After leaving their winter camp on April 7, 1805, the Corps continued up the Missouri River. However, they soon reached an impossible barrier: the Great Falls, in present-day Montana. The men had to carry their boats and supplies around the waterfalls on foot. This is called "portaging," and it took them one month to go only 18 miles (29 km).

The Great Falls of the Missouri River is where the journey began to be very difficult for the Corps. One of the few regrets Lewis expressed was not bringing a true artist along on the expedition, to paint the Great Falls.

Soon afterward, the Missouri River came to an end, and the Corps thought the Columbia River would take them to the Pacific Ocean—but they were wrong. They had to cross the Rocky Mountains first. Their only hope was to find the Shoshone Indians, who lived in the mountains, and buy horses from them, since crossing on foot was dangerous. Luckily, Sacagawea was able to introduce them to Cameahwait, the leader of the tribe. He was her brother, and he agreed to help. The Corps of Discovery was saved.

THE RETURN OF THE KEELBOAT

The keelboat became too large and heavy to continue upriver and was sent back down to St. Louis with its crew. Also on board were reports, maps, and samples of plants and animals— including a live prairie dog— for the president.

When Lewis and Clark would first meet a Native American tribe, the chief would be informed that the land now belonged to the U.S. and that Thomas Jefferson was the tribe's new "Great White Father."

PLANTS AND ANIMALS

As well as discovering a route west, Lewis and Clark had been instructed by Jefferson, in June 1803, to observe "the soil and face of the country, its growth and vegetable productions, the animals of the country generally, and especially those not known in the U.S."

Bitterroot was one of the foodplants gathered by the Shoshones. Its roots were boiled and eaten. Although Lewis thought it tasted terrible, the bitterroot was named for him, and in Latin is called Lewisia rediviva.

The Corps discovered 178 new plants on their expedition and collected dozens of specimens, which they carefully dried, pressed, and recorded.

Prairie dogs were one of the Corps' favorite animals on the trip. One day the men stopped the boats to study a huge prairie dog town that covered the land as far as they could see. They spent all day pouring river water down a hole trying to flush one of the animals out.

A GRIZZLY EXPERIENCE

One day Lewis went ashore and shot a buffalo. He suddenly noticed a grizzly bear moving toward him. He raised his gun to shoot but found he had no bullets. He tried to escape from the bear by jumping into the Medicine River, but the animal followed. Lewis turned to fight, and the bear suddenly ran away. Lewis recorded this narrow escape in his journal on June 14, 1805: "He pitched at me, open mouthed and full speed, I ran about 80 yards (73 m) and found he gained on me fast, I then [ran] into the water."

Patrick Gass wrote in his journal: "These [grizzly] bears are very bold and ferocious; and very large and powerful. The natives say they have killed a number of their brave men" (Tuesday, May 14, 1805). In this illustration by Gass, a bear has chased one of the men of the Corps up a tree.

Journey's End

After buying horses from the Shoshones, the Corps of Discovery decided to cross the Bitterroot Mountains in the Rocky Mountain range before winter. This was very bold, because if winter caught them in the mountains, they would surely die. A Shoshone known as "Old Toby" agreed to guide them. After a treacherous 11-day journey that brought them to the edge of starvation, they reached the other side and eventually found themselves sailing down the dangerous, fast-flowing Columbia River in their newly built dugout canoes.

Lewis and Clark camped at the source of the Columbia River and prepared to travel downriver to the Pacific Ocean. The Nez Percé Indians showed them how to make canoes by burning out the center of a log.

This fort was built to look exactly like Fort Clatsop, the winter home of the expedition in 1805. People can visit this fort today and imagine what it was like to live there so long ago.

They finally arrived at the Pacific Ocean on November 14, 1805, and built Fort Clatsop to live in during the cold and wet winter that followed. They kept themselves busy making new shirts, pants, and elk-hide moccasins for the long trip home and extracting salt out of ocean water. Lewis wrote constantly in his journals, and Clark drew his maps.

The Clatsop Hat

While staying at the fort, the Corps made contact with the local Clatsop Indians, who wore a style of hat that greatly impressed Lewis: *"We were visited today by two Clatsop women and two boys who brought a parsel [parcel] of excellent hats made of Cedar bark and ornamented with beargrass."*

Entry in Lewis's journal, February 22, 1806

23

THE TRIP HOME

On March 23, 1806, Lewis and Clark decided to leave the Pacific coast and start the long trip home to St. Louis.

The Rocky Mountains were huge barriers that were dangerous to cross. One day the Corps lost its supplies when a packhorse slipped on the trail and fell down the mountain.

The Corps needed Native American guides to take them back over the Rocky Mountains. Lewis suggested that the Corps split up and explore different routes on the return journey. They would meet where the Yellowstone and Missouri Rivers came together. On their trip, Lewis and his party met some Blackfeet Indians who tried to steal the Corps' rifles and horses. A fight started. Everyone fired their rifles at each other, and a bullet whizzed by close to Lewis's head. Lewis's men killed two Blackfoot warriors in the struggle.

Later on, Lewis had an accident. Pierre Cruzatte, the fiddler, couldn't see very well. He went out hunting, but accidentally shot Lewis in the rear end, mistaking him for an elk. Lewis recovered, however, and met Clark as planned the following day, and they finished the trip back down the Missouri River together.

When the Corps finally arrived in St. Louis, Missouri, on September 23, 1806, the people of the city were amazed. The Corps of Discovery had been gone so long that most people thought they were dead. In fact, only one Corps member died on the entire trip, and the rest returned home safe and sound.

When the Corps reached the Missouri River in 1806, the men knew they were nearing home. Sheheke, a Mandan chief, traveled on with them. He went to visit President Jefferson in the White House.

MAPPING THE EXPEDITION

Captains Lewis and Clark and the Corps of Discovery finished the longest ever exploration of the United States. They took a trip into dangerous territory covering over 8,000 miles (12,900 km) in 863 days (or 2 years and 4 months). They saw flat plains covered with grass and mountains covered with snow. They saw buffalo, grizzly bears, and prairie dogs. Captain Clark drew the first maps of this area, and they are still very accurate, even today.

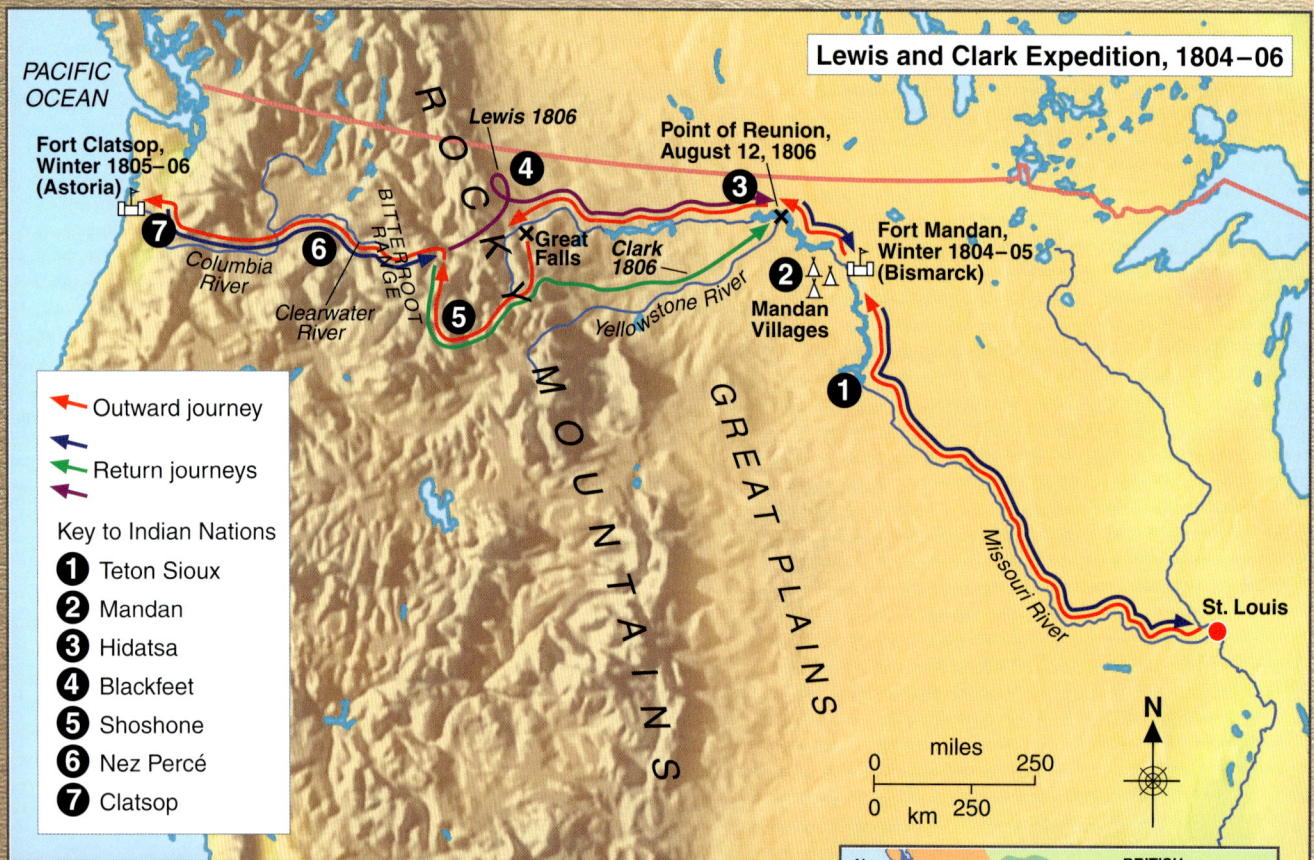

Lewis and Clark Expedition, 1804–06

PACIFIC OCEAN

Fort Clatsop, Winter 1805–06 (Astoria)

Lewis 1806

Point of Reunion, August 12, 1806

ROCKY MOUNTAINS

BITTERROOT RANGE

Great Falls

Clark 1806

Columbia River

Clearwater River

Yellowstone River

Fort Mandan, Winter 1804–05 (Bismarck)

Mandan Villages

GREAT PLAINS

Missouri River

St. Louis

Key
- ← Outward journey
- ← Return journeys
- ← Return journeys

Key to Indian Nations
1. Teton Sioux
2. Mandan
3. Hidatsa
4. Blackfeet
5. Shoshone
6. Nez Percé
7. Clatsop

miles 0 — 250
km 0 — 250

N

BRITISH TERRITORY

OREGON COUNTRY

Lewis and Clark Expedition 1804–1806

LOUISIANA PURCHASE

SPANISH TERRITORY

UNITED STATES

PACIFIC OCEAN

Mississippi River

This map shows the route taken by the Corps of Discovery from St. Louis to the Pacific Ocean and back again. Captains Lewis and Clark split up in the Rocky Mountains on the return journey and were reunited 5 weeks later.

In their journals, Lewis and Clark wrote about many animals that were new to science. These included the sage grouse, which Clark drew in his journal. He described it as smaller than a turkey, and good to eat.

Every day Lewis and Clark, and some of the other men, wrote about the trip in their journals, which were carried over mountains and floated down rivers. One day, Sacagawea jumped into the river to save the captains' journals when the boat carrying them overturned.

Clark was less educated than Lewis, and the spelling in his journal was very bad. Sergeant Patrick Gass wrote a journal, which is now missing. Charles Floyd, John Ordway, Joseph Whitehouse, and other members of the Corps, also kept journals, and there may be more journals that have not yet been discovered.

As well as their journals, Lewis and Clark collected and carefully pressed nearly 200 plant specimens from their trip. Amazingly, some of these can still be seen today at the Academy of Natural Sciences in Philadelphia.

THE LEGACY OF LEWIS AND CLARK

Meriwether Lewis and William Clark and their Corps of Discovery accomplished many things on their 1804–1806 expedition. Although they did not find an easy river route to the Pacific Ocean, Lewis and Clark did find the way and map it.

Many other people followed them to live in the West. Although white Americans benefited greatly from settling in these new territories, this began the decline of the Native American tribes, who eventually had their lands taken away from them.

This bronze statue of Lewis and Clark—with Sacagawea peering from behind—stands in Midway Park, Charlottesville, Virginia. It honors the two Virginia-born men who led the Corps of Discovery on its famous expedition.

BIRD NAMES

Following their expedition, both Lewis and Clark had birds named after them. Captain Lewis was honored in the naming of Lewis's woodpecker. Clark's nutcracker, a handsome gray and black bird of the crow family, was named after Captain Clark, who first recorded it in Idaho on August 22, 1805.

Lewis's woodpecker

Clark's nutcracker

The expedition made by the Corps helped science. Lewis and Clark identified 178 plants and 122 animals new to scientists. They wrote down important information about the country and the Native Americans who lived there. The most important and long-lasting result of the expedition were the journals that were written during the trip, and that can still be read today.

TIMELINE

1770–William Clark is born on August 1.

1774–Meriwether Lewis is born on August 18.

1801–Lewis becomes President Jefferson's personal secretary.

May 2, 1803–Louisiana Territory is purchased from France.

June 19, 1803–Lewis asks Clark to go on the journey with him.

July 1803–Lewis goes to Pittsburgh to prepare for the journey.

August 1803–Lewis leaves Pittsburgh with the keelboat to go to St. Louis.

December 1803–Lewis and Clark reach St. Louis and build Camp Wood as a winter camp.

May 14, 1804–Lewis and Clark leave Camp Wood and head up the Missouri River.

September 1804–Corps of Discovery meets the unfriendly Teton Sioux and sees the prairie dogs.

November 1804–The Corps builds Camp Mandan (winter camp) near Bismarck, ND.

April 7, 1805–The Corps leaves Camp Mandan to continue up the Missouri; the keelboat returns to St. Louis with specimens and some crew.

April 29, 1805–The Corps shoots its first grizzly bear.

June 1805–The Corps reaches Great Falls of the Missouri and portages around it.

August 1805–Lewis makes contact with the Shoshones in the Rocky Mountains.

October 7, 1805–The Corps reaches the Clearwater River on the other side of the mountains; boats used for the rest of the trip.

October 16, 1805–The Corps reaches the Columbia River.

November 7, 1805–The Corps sees the Pacific Ocean for the first time.

November 14, 1805–The Corps finally reaches the Pacific Ocean.

December 1805–The Corps builds Fort Clatsop (winter camp) near Astoria, Oregon.

March 23, 1806–The Corps starts home.

July 3, 1806–The expedition splits up; Lewis explores the Marias River, Clark the Yellowstone River.

July 27, 1806–Lewis's group kill two Blackfoot Indians in a fight.

August 11, 1806–Lewis is shot by accident.

August 12, 1806–The expedition is reunited on trip home.

September 23, 1806–Lewis and Clark reach St. Louis, finishing the expedition.

GLOSSARY

Barrier (BA-ree-ur) Something that blocks the way.

Corps (KOR) A group of people banded together; a troop.

Expedition (ek-spuh-DISH-uhn) A long trip.

Explore (ek-SPLOR) To find out about a new place.

Interpret (in-TUR-prit) to translate from one language to another.

Journal (JUR-nuhl) A diary or record of daily events.

Keelboat (KEEL-BOTE) A large, flat-bottomed riverboat.

Moccasins (MOK-uh-suhns) Shoes made from animal hides.

Nation (NAY-shuhn) A large group of people with their own government; a country or a tribe.

Navigate (NAV-uh-gate) To plan a route.

Nomadic (NOH-mad-ik) People who move from place to place.

Pirogue (PY-ROHG) A boat like a canoe.

Plantation (plan-TAY-shuhn) A large farm.

Portage (PORT-ij) To carry boats on land.

Specimen (SPESS-uh-muhn) A sample or example.

Wilderness (WIL-dur-niss) Land that is in its natural state.

FURTHER READING AND INFORMATION

Books to Read

Bergen, Lara. *The Travels of Lewis and Clark. (Explorers and Exploration)*. Austin, TX: Raintree Steck-Vaughn, 2000.

Bowen, Andy Russell. *The Back of Beyond: A Story About Lewis and Clark*. Minneapolis, MN: Carolrhoda Books, 1997.

Edwards, Judith. *Lewis and Clark's Journey of Discovery in American History*. Springfield, NJ: Enslow Publishers Inc., 1999.

Hall, Eleanor J. *The Lewis and Clark Expedition. (World History Series)*. San Diego, CA: Lucent Books, 1996.

Kiesling, Sanna Porte. *The Lewis and Clark Expedition. (Highlights from American History)*. Billings, MT: 1990.

Kozar, Richard. *Lewis and Clark: Explorers of the Louisiana Purchase*. Philadelphia: Chelsea House, 2000.

Kroll, Steven. *Lewis and Clark: Explorers of the American West*. New York: Holiday House, 1994.

Morley, Jacqueline. *Across America: The Story of Lewis and Clark*. New York: Franklin Watts, 1998.

Noonan, Jon. *Lewis and Clark*. New York: Crestwood House, 1993.

Roop, Peter and Connie (editors). *Off the Map: The Journals of Lewis and Clark*. New York: Walker and Co., 1993.

Schanzer, Rosalyn. *How We Crossed the West: The Adventures of Lewis and Clark*. Washington, D.C.: National Geographic Society, 1997.

Videos

Lewis and Clark: Explorers of the New Frontier. Greystone Communications, Inc. for A&E Television Networks, 1995.

Lewis and Clark: The Journey of the Corps of Discovery. Florentine Films and WETA-TV, 1997.

The Song of Sacagawea. Rabbit Ears Production, 1992.

"We Proceeded On": The Expedition of Lewis & Clark, 1804-1806. Lewis and Clark Trail Heritage Foundation, 1991.

INDEX